Doc Searls
David Weinberger

LE NUOVE TESI
DEL CLUETRAIN MANIFESTO

A CURA DI
Giulio Gaudiano

TITOLO ORIGINALE

NEW CLUES

CC BY-SA 3.0 IT 2015 YOUMEDIAWEB ROMA

WWW.YOUMEDIAWEB.COM

ISBN-13: 978-1507775165

ISBN-10: 1507775164

GRAZIE

Al Web perché mi ha dato il lavoro che sognavo.

A Robin Good perché mi ha fatto conoscere il Cluetrain Manifesto e mi ha insegnato la strada per la foresta di Sharewood.

Ai miei soci e collaboratori, perché sono i migliori compagni di avventure.

A mia moglie, perché tiene a bada il geek che è in me.

INTRODUZIONE

Il contesto.

Nel 1999 la maggior parte dei Media vedeva il Web come un nuovo canale per spingere contenuti. Il mondo business, dal canto suo, intravedeva l'opportunità di vendere di più. Il resto delle persone però, aveva davanti un altro Internet, luogo ideale per inventare nuove cose, per condividerle liberamente, per incontrarsi e comunicare senza limiti.

Quattro di queste persone, stanche dei continui fraintendimenti circa la vera natura di Internet, tentarono di dipingere l'immagine della Rete che conoscevano e amavano scrivendo 95 tesi, raccolte nel Cluetain Manifesto[1].

Erano solo in quattro: Doc Searls[2] e David Weinberger[3] (autori del testo che stai per leggere), Christopher Locke[4] e Rick Levine[5]. Eppure quel testo fu letto da centinaia di migliaia di persone online e, come libro[6], divenne un best-seller.

---

1   http://www.cluetrain.com/
2   http://searls.com/
3   http://weinberger.org/
4   http://www.cluetrain.com/clocke.html
5   https://www.linkedin.com/in/ricklevine
6   A dieci anni dalla pubblicazione del Cluetrain Manifesto è stato pubblicato un volume arricchito di interventi e

Da allora è passata molta acqua sotto i ponti.
Quindici anni dopo Doc e David, che nel frattempo
hanno scritto vari libri e ricoprono posti di prestigio
nel mondo accademico, danno nuovamente voce
all'Internet Libero, affinché chi ne abbia smarrito la
via possa aprire gli occhi e aggiustare la propria
rotta.

Il testo.

Il testo che stai per leggere è una profezia su
Internet. Da qui il suo tono fortemente visionario e
religioso.

"Ascolta, Internet" esordisce. Come il popolo di
Israele, sotto il monte Oreb, riceve da Dio delle
parole per essere felice e prendere possesso della
Terra Promessa[7], così David Weinberger e Doc
Searls indicano la strada che permetterà al Popolo
della Rete di attraversare un deserto popolato di
orde di predoni, per entrare infine nella terra
dell'Open Internet.

Lo stesso David Weinberger ha riconosciuto di non
essere un ebreo praticante, ma di aver voluto
comunque celare nel testo numerosi Easter egg[8] e

---

riflessioni: http://cluetrain.com/Cluetrain_10/

7   L'incipit del testo fa eco al brano di Deuteronomio 6,3
    "Ascolta, o Israele, e bada di metterli in pratica; perché tu
    sia felice e cresciate molto di numero nel paese dove
    scorre il latte e il miele, come il Signore, Dio dei tuoi
    padri, ti ha detto."

8   http://it.wikipedia.org/wiki/Easter_egg

richiami allo stile dei testi rabbinici e sapienziali[9].

La formattazione, che ho voluto conservare il più fedelmente possibile, è frutto di un'attenzione particolare, degna della poesia visiva[10].

Il copyright.

Il testo originale è stato pubblicato su http://cluetrain.com/newclues/[11]

La traduzione che leggerai in questo libro è stata scritta da Giulio Gaudiano, rielaborando l'ottima traduzione di Andrea Zanni, Marco Goldin ed Enrico Francese[12]

Questo libro può essere condiviso, distribuito, comunicato al pubblico, rappresentato e recitato con qualsiasi mezzo e formato; modificato, remixato, utilizzato in qualsiasi modo, ricordando sempre l'autore e utilizzando la stessa licenza[13].

Facci quello che ti pare, ma facci qualcosa. :-)

---

9   Cfr. Intervista a David Weinberger di Marco Montemagno, trasmessa in diretta il 21 gennaio 2015 su http://supersummit.co/
10 http://it.wikipedia.org/wiki/Poesia_visiva
11 Il testo è pubblicato sotto Pubblico Dominio CC0 1.0
12 Il testo su https://medium.com/@nuovetesi/nuove-tesi-4a1def360351è pubblicato sotto licenza Creative Commons CC BY-SA 3.0 IT
13 https://creativecommons.org/licenses/by-sa/3.0/it/

NUOVE TESI

http://cluetrain.com/newclues/

Ascolta, Internet.[14]

Sono passati quindici anni dal nostro precedente messaggio[15].

A quel tempo la Gente di Internet – io, te e tutti i nostri amici degli amici degli amici, fino all'ultimo Kevin Bacon[16] —ha fatto di Internet un luogo stupendo, pieno di meraviglie e di portenti.

Dalle cose serie[17] a quelle scherzose[18] fino alle più assurde[19], abbiamo distrutto giganti, creato eroi e modificato le più semplici convinzioni su Chi Siamo e Come Va il Mondo.

Ma adesso, tutto il buon lavoro fatto insieme sta per affrontare pericoli mortali.

Quando ci siamo rivolti a te per la prima volta, volevamo metterti in guardia della minaccia rappresentata da chi non capiva di non aver capito Internet.

Questi sono "Gli Stolti", i business che hanno

---

14 N.d.t. L'incipit fa eco alla preghiera ebraica Shemà, la quale inizia recitando "Ascolta, Israele". Cfr. http://it.wikipedia.org/wiki/Shemà

15 http://www.cluetrain.com/

16 N.d.t. Il nome di Kevin Bacon contiene un'allusione alla teoria dei sei gradi di separazione. Cfr. http://it.wikipedia.org/wiki/Sei_gradi_di_separazione

17 http://en.wikipedia.org/

18 http://lolcatbible.com/

19 http://www.truthforhumanity.com/

semplicemente fatto proprie le trappole di Internet.

Ora due nuove orde minacciano quello che noi abbiamo costruito l'uno per l'altro.

I Marauders[20] capiscono Internet fin troppo bene. Pensano che appartenga a loro e che possano depredarlo, prelevando da esso i nostri dati e i nostri soldi, convinti che noi siamo cretini.

Ma l'orda più pericolosa è la terza: Noi.

Un'orda è una massa indifferenziata di persone. Ma la vera essenza di Internet è che ci permette di connetterci, in quanto individui diversi e distinti.

A tutti noi piace l'intrattenimento di massa. Diamine, al giorno d'oggi la TV ne sta facendo delle belle, e la Rete ci permette di guardarcele quando ci pare. Fantastico!

Ma dobbiamo tenere a mente, che trasmettere mass media è solo l'ultimo dei poteri della Rete.

Il super-potere della Rete è la connessione senza bisogno di autorizzazione. Il suo massimo potere è che possiamo fare di essa quello che ci pare.

Dunque non è il momento di metterci comodi e consumare il ma-che-buon cibo spazzatura che Stolti e Marauders hanno creato, come se il nostro lavoro fosse finito. È il momento di soffiare sul fuoco della Rete e trasformare tutte le istituzioni

---

20 I Marauders sono un gruppo di supercriminali mutanti dei fumetti, creati da Chris Claremont (testi), John Romita Jr. (disegni). Cfr. http://it.wikipedia.org/wiki/Marauders

che vorrebbero prenderci in giro.

E' già iniziata l'invasione sistematica di Internet da parte degli ultracorpi[21]. Non fare errori: con un tratto di penna, una stretta di mano segreta o permettendo ai meme di coprire le grida dei più disperati, rischiamo di perdere l'Internet che amiamo.

Ci siamo rivolti a te negli anni della nascita del Web. Siamo invecchiati insieme a Internet. Il tempo che ci rimane è poco.

Noi, il Popolo di Internet, dobbiamo ricordare la gloria della sua rivelazione, per poterlo rivendicare ora in nome di ciò che è veramente.

David Weinberger

Doc Searls

8 gennaio, 2015

---

21 http://en.wikipedia.org/wiki/Invasion_of_the_Body_Snatc hers. Cfr. http://it.wikipedia.org/wiki/L %27invasione_degli_Ultracorpi_(film)

UN TEMPO ERAVAMO GIOVANI NEL GIARDINO…

a. Internet siamo noi, connessi.

1. Internet non è fatto di cavi, di fibre ottiche, di onde radio e neanche di tubi.

2. I dispositivi che usiamo, per connetterci a Internet, non sono Internet.

3. Verizon, Comcast, AT&T, Deutsche Telekom e 中国电信 non possiedono Internet. Facebook, Google e Amazon non sono i re della Rete, né lo sono i loro servitori o i loro algoritmi. Né i governi della terra né le loro Associazioni per il Commercio hanno il consenso dei connessi[22] per cavalcare la Rete come sovrani.

4. Internet è un nostro bene comune, non una nostra proprietà.

5. Da noi e da quello che abbiamo costruito su di esso deriva tutto il valore di Internet.

6. La Rete è di noi, da noi, per noi.

7. Internet è nostro.

b. Internet non è niente, e non serve a niente.

8. Internet non è una cosa, più di quanto non lo

---

22 http://consentofthenetworked.com/

sia la forza di gravità. Entrambe ci tengono insieme.

9. Internet è una totale non-cosa. Alla sua base c'è un insieme di accordi, che i più nerd fra noi (benedetti siano i loro nomi nei secoli) chiamano "protocolli", ma che noi potremmo, nel fervore del momento, chiamare "comandamenti."

10. Il primo e il più importante è: La tua rete muoverà i pacchetti a destinazione senza favoritismi o ritardi in base a origine, sorgente, contenuto o intenzione.

11. Possa dunque questo Primo Comandamento aprire Internet a ogni idea, applicazione, business, avventura, vizio o qualsiasi altra cosa.

12. Non si è mai visto uno strumento così generalmente utilizzabile dall'invenzione del linguaggio.

13. Questo significa che Internet non è fatto per qualcosa in particolare. Non è fatto per i social network, né per i documenti, né per la pubblicità, né per il business, né per l'educazione, né per il porno, né per qualsiasi altra cosa. È adatto nello specifico a fare qualsiasi cosa.

14. Ottimizzare[23] Internet per una singola cosa

23 http://books.google.com/books?
id=9lTtWQlLkwwC&pg=PA56&lpg=PA56&dq=optimizi

significa de-ottimizzarlo per tutto il resto.

15. Internet, come la gravità, è indiscriminato. Ci tiene insieme, giusti e ingiusti allo stesso modo[24].

c. La Rete non è contenuto.

16. Su Internet ci sono contenuti fantastici. Ma, maremma formaggina[25], Internet non è fatto di contenuti.

17. La prima poesia di un adolescente, la tanto attesa rivelazione di un segreto custodito a lungo; un bel disegno buttato giù da una mano paralitica; il post di un blog in un regime politico che odia il suono delle voci del suo popolo: nessuna di queste persone aveva intenzione di creare un contenuto.

18. Abbiamo usato la parola "contenuto" senza

---

ng+de-optimizing+david+reed&source=bl&ots=_mqGSLoqSV&sig=TWO4uUTWkzGPDBGmwyS0uqBz0NA&hl=en&sa=X&ei=Nm5lVN-hJtbdsASnzoKQAQ&ved=0CCAQ6AEwAA#v=onepage&q=optimizing%20de-optimizing%20david%20reed&f=false

24 N.d.t. Nel testo originale questa affermazione potrebbe essere un easter egg di una novella di Samuel Johnson "The angels of affliction spread their toils alike for the virtuous and the wicked, for the mighty and the mean".

25 N.d.t. Libera interpretazione dell'esclamazione "holy mother of cheeses".

virgolette? Ce ne vergogniamo.

d. La Rete non è un medium.

19. La Rete non è un medium più di quanto non lo sia una conversazione.

20. Sulla Rete, il medium siamo noi. Noi portiamo i messaggi. Lo facciamo ogni volta che pubblichiamo un post, ritwittiamo, mandiamo un link in una email o lo postiamo su un social network.

21. Contrariamente a un medium, tu ed io lasciamo le nostre impronte digitali, e talvolta il segno dei denti, sui messaggi che passiamo. Diciamo alle persone perché mandiamo quel messaggio. Lo rafforziamo. Vi aggiungiamo una battuta. Tagliamo la parte che non ci piace. Ci appropriamo di questi messaggi.

22. Tutte le volte che portiamo un messaggio attraverso la Rete, esso porta con sé un piccolo pezzo di noi.

23. Portiamo un messaggio attraverso questo "medium", solo se esso è importante per noi, in uno qualsiasi degli infiniti modi in cui gli esseri umani possono avere a cuore qualcosa.

24. Avere a cuore—ritenere importante—è la forza motrice di Internet.

e. Il Web è World Wide.

25. Nel 1991, Tim Berners-Lee[26] usò la Rete per creare un regalo, che donò gratis a tutti noi: il World Wide Web. Grazie.

26. Tim ha creato il Web fornendo dei protocolli (di nuovo questa parola!) che dicono come scrivere una pagina che può linkare a un'altra pagina senza chiedere il permesso a nessuno.

27. Boom. Nel giro di dieci anni abbiamo avuto miliardi di pagine sul Web: un 'impresa collettiva delle dimensioni di una Guerra Mondiale, e tuttavia così positiva che la più grande lamentela è stata per il tag <blink>.

28. Il Web è un regno gigantesco e semi-eterno, fatto di cose da scoprire nelle loro fitte inter-connessioni.

29. Questa l'ho già sentita. Ma certo, è esattamente come il mondo reale.

30. Diversamente dal mondo reale, ogni cosa e ogni connessione sul Web è stata creata da qualcuno di noi, mostrando un interesse e un punto di vista su come piccoli pezzi[27] si combinano tra loro.

31. Ogni link creato da una persona, con

---

26 http://en.wikipedia.org/wiki/Tim_Berners-Lee
27 http://www.smallpieces.com/

qualcosa da dire, è un atto di generosità e altruismo, che invita i lettori a lasciare la pagina dove stanno, per guardare il mondo dal punto di vista di qualcun'altro.

32. Il Web ricrea il mondo nella nostra forma feconda e condivisa[28].

---

28 N.d.t. La traduzione dell'originale "The Web remakes the world in our collective, emergent image." è in accordo con lo stile biblico del testo. Secondo le intenzioni degli autori il Web sembra capace di ricreare la realtà del giardino dell'Eden, in cui tutto era in continua crescita e fioritura e, non esistendo la proprietà privata, tutto era per tutti e di tutti. Tale interpretazione è rafforzata dal fatto che questa affermazione chiude, secondo una composizione ad anello, la sezione del testo iniziata con "Once were we young in the Garden...".

MA AHIMÈ, COME ABBIAMO
POTUTO ALLONTANARCENE,
FRATELLI E SORELLE…

a. Tuttavia, come abbiamo potuto lasciare che la conversazione fosse trasformata in un'arma[29]?

33. È importante riconoscere e aver cura del dialogo, dell'amicizia e dei mille gesti di empatia, gentilezza e gioia che incontriamo su Internet.

34. E ancora sentiamo le parole "frocio" e "negro" molto più in Rete che fuori.

35. La demonizzazione degli 'altri'—persone con look, linguaggi, opinioni, appartenenze o altri modi di stare insieme che non capiamo, apprezziamo o tolleriamo— su Internet è peggiore che mai.

36. Le donne in Arabia Saudita non possono guidare? Nel frattempo, metà di noi[30] non può parlare liberamente sulla Rete senza doversi guardare alle spalle[31].

37. C'è odio in Rete perché c'è odio nel mondo, ma la Rete rende più facile la sua espressione e il suo ascolto.

---

29 http://blog.bl00cyb.org/2014/11/akirachix-and-weaponized-social/

30 https://medium.com/message/online-and-offline-violence-towards-women-4c854eb591a5

31 http://www.theguardian.com/technology/2013/aug/05/twitter-bomb-threats-women

38. La soluzione: se avessimo una soluzione, non staremmo qui a scocciare con tutte queste dannate tesi.

39. Possiamo però dire questo: non è stato l'odio a creare la Rete, ma sta portando la Rete—e tutti noi—indietro.

40. Ammettiamo almeno che la Rete ha i suoi valori impliciti. Valori umani.

41. Ad uno sguardo freddo la Rete è solo tecnologia. Ma è popolata da creature che si scaldano per quello a cui tengono: le loro vite, i loro amici, il mondo che condividiamo.

42. La Rete ci offre un luogo condiviso dove possiamo essere noi stessi, insieme ad altri che apprezzano le nostre differenze.

43. Nessuno è padrone di questo luogo. Tutti possono usarlo. Chiunque può migliorarlo.

44. Ecco cos'è un Internet libero. Sono state combattute guerre per molto meno.

b. "Siamo d'accordo su tutto. Ti trovo *affascinante!*"

45. Il mondo ci si offre davanti come un buffet, eppure noi vogliamo sempre la nostra bistecca con patate, l'agnello con hummus, il pesce con riso, o qualsiasi altra cosa.

46. Facciamo così in parte perché la conversazione ha bisogno di un terreno comune: linguaggi, interessi, regole, punti di vista condivisi. Senza di questi è difficile, se non impossibile, avere una conversazione.

47. Terreni comuni generano tribù. Il Mondo con la sua dura terra ha tenuto a distanza le tribù, permettendo loro di sviluppare incredibili diversità. Evviva! Le tribù hanno fatto crescere il Noi invece del Loro e della guerra. Evviva? Mica tanto.

48. Su Internet, la distanza tra le tribù parte da zero.

49. Apparentemente, essere capaci di trovarci l'un l'altro interessanti non è così semplice come sembra.

50. Questa è una sfida che possiamo affrontare essendo aperti, empatici e pazienti.
Possiamo farcela ragazzi! Siamo i numeri 1!
Siamo i numeri 1!

51. Essere accoglienti: ecco un valore che la Rete ha bisogno di imparare dalle nostre migliori culture del mondo reale.

c. Il marketing rende ancora più difficile parlare.

52. Avevamo ragione la prima volta[32]: i Mercati sono conversazioni.

53. Conversazione non significa tirarci per la manica, per mostrarci un prodotto di cui non vogliamo sentir parlare.

54. Se vogliamo sapere la verità sui vostri prodotti, la scopriremo da qualcun'altro.

55. Ci rendiamo conto che queste conversazioni sono incredibilmente interessanti per voi. Peccato. Sono nostre.

56. Se volete partecipare alla nostra conversazione siete i benvenuti, ma solo se ci dite per chi lavorate e se potete parlare in modo autonomo e personale.

57. Tutte le volte che ci chiamate "consumatori", ci sentiamo come mucche che cercano il significato della parola "carne".

58. Smettetela di trivellare le nostre esistenze per estrarre dati che non vi riguardano e che le vostre macchine interpretano male.

59. Non preoccupatevi: vi diremo noi quando scenderemo sul mercato per qualche motivo. A modo nostro. Non vostro. Fidatevi: sarà

---

32 http://www.cluetrain.com/

meglio per voi[33].

60. Gli annunci pubblicitari che suonano umani ma provengono dagli intestini irritabili del vostro ufficio marketing, macchiano la stoffa del Web.

61. Quando la personalizzazione porta a cose raccapriccianti, è un chiaro segnale che non capite cosa significa veramente essere una persona.

62. Umano è Personale. Non Personalizzato.

63. Più le macchine sembrano umane, più scivolano nella uncanny valley[34] dove ogni cosa è raccapricciante[35] .

64. E poi: smettetela di travestire gli annunci

---

33 http://intentioneconomy.net/
34 https://en.wikipedia.org/wiki/Uncanny_valley N.d.t.
Uncanny valley (traduzione: la zona perturbante o valle perturbante) è un'ipotesi presentata dallo studioso di robotica nipponico Masahiro Mori nel 1970 pubblicata sulla rivista Energy. La ricerca analizza sperimentalmente come la sensazione di familiarità e di piacevolezza generata in un campione di persone da robot e automi antropomorfi aumenti al crescere della loro somiglianza con la figura umana fino ad un punto in cui l'estremo realismo rappresentativo produce però un brusco calo delle reazioni emotive positive, destando sensazioni spiacevoli come repulsione e inquietudine paragonabili al perturbamento. Cfr.
https://it.wikipedia.org/wiki/Uncanny_valley
35 http://www.niemanlab.org/2014/12/the-year-we-get-creeped-out-by-algorithms/

pubblicitari da news, nella speranza che non ci accorgiamo dell'etichetta appesa alle loro mutande.

65. Quando fate "native advertising" non solo intaccate la vostra stessa credibilità, ma anche la credibilità di tutto questo nuovo modo di entrare in relazione gli uni con gli altri.

66. A proposito, che ne dite di chiamare la "native advertising" con uno dei suoi veri nomi come "product placement", "pubbliredazionali", o "notizie finte del cazzo"?

67. Gli inserzionisti sono andati avanti per generazioni senza essere raccapriccianti. Possono cavarsela senza essere raccapriccianti anche sulla Rete.

d. La Gitmo[36] della Rete.

68. Tutti amiamo le nostre scintillanti app,

---

36 N.d.t. Il termine "Gitmo" può essere letto come sinonimo di "Guantanamo", struttura detentiva statunitense di massima sicurezza interna alla base navale di Guantánamo, sull'isola di Cuba. *Gitmo - Le nuove regole della guerra* (*Gitmo: Krigets nya spelregler*), noto anche con il titolo internazionale *Gitmo: The New Rules of War*, è un documentario svedese pubblicato nel 2006 da Erik Gandini e Tarik Saleh. Cfr. http://it.wikipedia.org/wiki/Gitmo_-_Le_nuove_regole_della_guerra

anche quando sono blindate quanto una base lunare. Ma se metti insieme tutte le app blindate del mondo avrai soltanto un mucchio di app.

69. Metti insieme tutte le pagine del Web e avrai un nuovo mondo.

70. Le pagine web creano connessioni. Le app, controllo.

71. Se passiamo dal Web[37] ad un mondo fatto di app[38], perdiamo tutto ciò che di condiviso stavamo costruendo insieme.

72. Nel Regno delle App siamo utenti, non creatori.

73. Ogni nuova pagina rende il Web più grande. Ogni nuovo link rende il Web più ricco.

74. Ogni nuova app ci dà qualcos'altro da fare sull'autobus.

75. Ahi, un colpo basso!

76. Ehi, "ColpoBasso" potrebbe essere il nome per una nuova app! Già me la immagino, con su scritto "Acquistala nell'App Store".

---

37 http://dashes.com/anil/2012/12/rebuilding-the-web-we-lost.html
38 https://indiewebcamp.com/Principles

e. La gravità è una gran cosa, fino a quando non ci risucchia tutti in un buco nero.

77. Le applicazioni non-libere[39] sviluppate a scapito della Rete libera stanno diventando inevitabili, quanto la forza di attrazione di un buco nero.

78. Se per te la Rete è Facebook, allora ti sono stati messi addosso degli occhiali da un'azienda che ha la responsabilità, nei confronti dei suoi azionisti, di impedirti di toglierli.

79. Google, Amazon, Facebook e Apple fanno tutte il business degli occhiali. La prima verità, che i loro occhiali nascondono, è che queste aziende vogliono impossessarsi di noi proprio come i buchi neri si impossessano della luce.

80. Queste singolarità aziendali sono pericolose, non perché sono cattive. Molte di loro infatti sono impegnate in ottime iniziative di pubblica utilità. Dovrebbero essere applaudite per questo.

81. Ma esse traggono beneficio dall'attrazione gravitazionale della socialità: l'"effetto network" è quello che si verifica quando

39 https://medium.com/message/net-neutrality-is-sooo-much-more-than-access-to-the-tubes-2344b1e9f220

molti usano qualcosa perché è già usato da molti.

82. Dove non ci sono alternative competitive, dobbiamo stare iper-attenti, per ricordare a questi Giganti della Valley i valori del Web che all'inizio li hanno ispirati.

83. E poi abbiamo bisogno di onorare il suono che facciamo quando uno di noi si allontana coraggiosamente da loro. E' un suono a metà tra il boato di un razzo, in partenza dalla piattaforma di lancio, e lo strappo del Velcro quando ci si slaccia un vestito troppo stretto.

f. La privacy nell'era delle spie.

84. Ok governi, avete vinto. Avete in mano i nostri dati. Ora, cosa possiamo fare per assicurarci che userete questi dati contro di Loro e non contro di Noi? Anzi, sapreste dirci che differenza c'è?

85. Se vogliamo che i nostri governi facciano un passo indietro, dobbiamo accettare che se – e quando – ci sarà un nuoco attacco, non ci potremo poi lamentare, dicendo che avrebbero dovuto sorvegliarci meglio.

86. Non c'è scambio equo, se non siamo consapevoli di quello a cui rinunciamo. Non hai mai sentito dire che per la Sicurezza

bisogna rinunciare alla Privacy?

87. Con una probabilità, che si avvicina
all'assoluta certezza, ci pentiremo di non
aver fatto di più per proteggere nostri i dati
dalle mani dei governi e dai signori supremi
delle grandi aziende.

g. La privacy nell'era dei disonesti.

88. È giusto garantire la privacy personale a chi
la vuole. Tutti stabiliamo dei limiti a un
certo punto.

89. Domanda: Quanto pensi ci sia voluto
affinché la cultura pre-Web capisse dove
stabilire i limiti? Risposta: "Quanti anni ha
questa cultura?"

90. Il Web è appena uscito dall'adolescenza. Ci
troviamo all'inizio, non alla fine, della storia
della privacy.

91. Potremo comprendere che cosa vuol dire
privato, solo quando avremo capito cosa
vuol dire social. Abbiamo appena iniziato a
reinventare questi concetti.

92. Gli incentivi economici e politici, per farci
abbassare i pantaloni e sollevare la gonna,
sono così forti che faremmo meglio a
investire in mutande di stagnola.

93. Sono gli hacker ad averci portato a questo,

gli hacker dovranno tirarcene fuori.

PER COSTRUIRE E SEMINARE

a. Kumbaya[40] è bellissima se sei in una cassa di risonanza.

94. Internet è sbalorditivo[41]. Il Web è fantastico. Tu sei bellissimo. Connettiamoci tutti e saremo più incredibilmente meravigliosi di Jennifer Lawrence[42]. È un dato di fatto.

95. E allora, non sminuiamo quello che la Rete ha fatto negli ultimi vent'anni.

96. C'è molta più musica in giro per il mondo.

97. Ora siamo in grado di farci una cultura da soli, salvo occasionali incursioni al cinema per qualcosa di spumeggiante e una busta di pop-corn da 9 dollari.

98. Ora i politici devono spiegare le loro posizioni in modo ben diverso rispetto al vecchio volantino elettorale ciclostilato[43].

---

40 N.d.t. Kumbaya è una canzone che dagli anni '20 cominciò a circolare negli ambienti Scout e durante i campi estivi. La canzone è una semplice preghiera a Dio affinché aiuti chi è in difficoltà, ma è diventata un modo per alludere in modo satirico ad una visione moralistica, ipocrita e ingenuamente ottimistica del mondo e della natura umana. Cfr. http://en.wikipedia.org/wiki/Kumbaya

41 http://www.reddit.com/r/internetisbeautiful

42 Jennifer Lawrence è stata definita dalla rivista Rolling Stone "la più talentuosa giovane attrice di tutta l'America". Cfr. http://it.wikipedia.org/wiki/Jennifer_Lawrence

43 http://en.wikipedia.org/wiki/Mimeograph

99. Per tutto ciò che non capisci, puoi trovare una spiegazione. Puoi parlarne con altri. Puoi persino litigarci. Non è evidente quanto tutto ciò sia fantastico?

100. Vuoi sapere cosa comprare? L'ultimo a cui chiedere è quel business che fa di tutto per creare un oggetto del desiderio. La migliore fonte di informazioni siamo noi tutti.

101. Vuoi un corso di livello universitario su un argomento che ti interessa? Cerca su Google[44]. Scegline uno. È gratis.

102. Certo, Internet non ha risolto tutti i problemi del mondo. Ecco perché l'Onnipotente ci ha fatto dono delle chiappe: per farcele alzare dalla sedia.

103. Gli oppositori di Internet ci aiutano a mantenerci onesti. Ma li apprezziamo di più quando loro stessi non si comportano da ingrati.

b. Una tasca piena di buone intenzioni.

104. Stavamo per dirvi come aggiustare Internet in quattro semplici mosse, ma l'unica che ci

---

44 http://www.bing.com/search?q=google N.d.t. Questo link è una sorta di corto circuito. Per riferirsi a Google gli autori non linkano il motore di ricerca, bensì linkano la ricerca della parola "Google" su Bing, motore di ricerca suo principale concorrente.

viene in mente è l'ultima: il profitto[45]. Così, invece, ecco alcuni pensieri sparsi...

105. Dovremmo sostenere gli artisti e i creativi che ci danno gioia o ci fanno sentire più leggeri.

106. Dovremmo avere il coraggio di chiedere[46] l'aiuto di cui abbiamo bisogno.

107. La nostra cultura porta naturalmente alla condivisione, mentre la legge porta naturalmente alla difesa del copyright. Il copyright ha la sua funzione, ma nel dubbio, open[47] è meglio .

108. Nel contesto sbagliato sono tutti str--zi. (Anche noi, ma lo sapevate già). Perciò se inviti le persone a fare una nuotata, stabilisci prima delle regole. Tutti i troll, fuori dalla piscina.

109. Se le conversazioni sul tuo sito prendono una brutta piega, la colpa è tua.

110. Laddove c'è una conversazione, nessuno è tenuto a risponderti, non importa quanto sia condivisibile il tuo punto di vista o quanto smagliante sia il tuo sorriso.

111. Sostieni le aziende che hanno davvero capito il Web. Le riconoscerai non tanto

---

45 http://knowyourmeme.com/memes/profit
46 http://www.ted.com/speakers/amanda_palmer
47 http://www.creativecommons.org/

perché ci assomigliano, ma perché sono dalla nostra parte.

112. Certo, le app offrono una bella esperienza. Ma il Web è fatto di collegamenti che si diramano in continuazione, connettendoci senza fine. Per la vita e le idee, la completezza è la morte. Scegli la vita.

113. La rabbia è la patente della stupidità. Le strade di Internet sono già troppo affollate di guidatori patentati.

114. Vivi i valori che vuoi promuovere su Internet.

115. Se è un po' che parli, prova a star zitto. (Tra poco lo faremo anche noi).

c. Stare insieme: la causa e la soluzione di ogni problema[48].

116. Se ci siamo concentrati sul ruolo del Popolo della Rete — tu e noi —nel declino di Internet, è perché conserviamo ancora la stessa fede che avevamo all'inizio.

117. Noi, il Popolo della Rete, non riusciamo a comprendere quanto si possa fare insieme, perché siamo ancora lontani dall'aver finito di inventare come stare insieme.

---

48 http://en.wikipedia.org/wiki/Homer_vs._the_Eighteenth_A mendment

118. Internet ha liberato una forza primordiale — la gravità in grado di tenerci insieme.

119. L'amore è la forza di gravità della connessione.

120. Lunga vita a Internet libero.

121. Che si possa avere a lungo un Internet da amare.

AUTORI

Doc Searls

David "Doc" Searls, nato nel 1947, autore di *The Intention Economy: When Customers Take Charge*, è un giornalista, editorialista e blogger.

Membro del Center for Information Technology & Society (CITS) presso l'Università della California a Santa Barbara e del Berkman Center for Internet & Society presso l'Università di Harvard.

Per saperne di più http://searls.com/

David Weinberger

Nato nel 1950 e autore di *Everything is miscellaneous: the power of the new digital disorder* e di *Too Big to Know: Rethinking Knowledge Now That the Facts Aren't the Facts, Experts Are Everywhere*, è un tecnologo della comunicazione, scrittore e filosofo.

E' membro del Berkman Center for Internet & Society presso l'Università di Harvard, dove co-dirige anche l'Harvard Library Innovation Lab.

Per saperne di più http://weinberger.org/

Giulio Gaudiano

Nato nel 1983 e autore di *Esperto YouTube: Come Guadagnare con i Video Online*, è imprenditore e consulente di marketing, editoria e business digitale.

Per saperne di più http://giuliogaudiano.com/

alerts between both states. Accomplishing this involves the utilization of a separate API token for non-production and production that reports to a selected APM solution, or the modification of alert policy programmatically on an environment's APM, with a changed role.

- **Automate**

  Automating tasks during the switching process brings many benefits than manually performing those same actions. Since it is automated, the switch will occur quicker, it will be easier, safer (as executing tasks manually is more prone to error), and can be performed by authorized persons.

- **Create compatible code** Since old versions and new versions of the code are implementing simultaneously throughout the switch exercise, co-existence of both versions is key.

o **Canary deployment:** is a method that operates in a phased approach by deploying new code in a little section of the production environment. As soon as the application is approved for release, a small number of users are directed to it. Thereby reducing any impact. If there are no defects reported, the new version is steadily rolled out to the remaining sections of the environment. Canary deployment can cover any type of application – mobile, desktop or website, as well as different infrastructures – hybrid, cloud or on premise.

The foremost obstacle of canary deployment is to find an approach to direct a few users to the newly deployed application. There may be instances where some applications require similar collection of users for testing, whereas others may need a diverse collection of users each time.

There are several techniques to explore when looking for a way to direct users, these include:

- Operating an application inference to reveal new features to specific groups and users. When the new release is available for the remaining users, the inference is removed;
- Deploying the application in specific regions;
- Direct the users based on the source IP range;
- Carry out canary development with internal users before giving access to external users.

Canary deployments can operate on varying infrastructures, for example:

- **Load balancers**
  Even though canary deployment can be

performed without applying load balancers, it is just simpler as the server needing update can be taken out of the cycle. In this instance, there are two load balancers, where load balancer X will accept ninety percent of the traffic flow, while load balancer Y gets the other ten percent. Load balancer Y will be for canary deployments, denoting that the servers following it will first be updated. After this, testing and monitoring can be put in place for some time. If the outcome in load balancer X is not desirable, rollback and complete the release. Else, advance to upgrade the servers following load balancer Y.

- **Amazon Web Services (AWS)**

  Route 53, a service of AWS, allows weighted registers to divide the traffic. If there is no intention to involve DNS TTLs, utilize Auto-Scaling Groups (ASG). An interesting information about ASG is that no matter the number of ASGs, there is a requisite for only a single Elastic Load Balancer (ELB) since every ASG attaches to the same ELB, thus stabilizing the load amongst ASGs. Canary deployments with

ASGs administers similar approach, with a little modification. The Amazon Machine Image (AMI) that contains the additional modifications will be wielded to update the ASG and swap the existing instance with the new. The new instance can be launched first without having to worry about downtime. As soon as the instance is recorded in the load balancer, connections in the old instance can be drained and ended. Using this approach, rollback involves modifying the ASG with the preceding AMI

and swap instances
thereafter.

- **Kubernetes**
The technique used here is
comparable to that of
Amazon Web Services, but
with different phrasing of
terms. There is a service
that is considered as a load
balancer for pods installed
here, as well as
"deployments" that behave
like ASGs.

- **Containers**
Containers are utilized to
package the application
dependencies and code, for
easier movement of the
application. It is quite easy
to implement containers
using Docker by using

Dockerfile and defining the commands and dependencies for the application there. The Dockerfile creates Docker Image, and utilizes it to instantiate a container.

The DevOps Engineer

In the traditional model, software developers write codes for a period and gives the completed work to the QA team for testing, after which the operations team receives the final release for deployment. There is a noted absence of collaboration between the stages of development, testing and deployment. Software developers create the code and transfers the completed code to the deployment team. Thereafter, it is either left to the deployment team to resolve the issues that come up all through code deployment or it is returned to the development team to correct the issue. This leads to slowdowns in the software development process.

However, in the DevOps model, this is no longer the case, as these teams will not be apart. In most cases, these teams are grouped as one team where the DevOps engineers operates through the complete lifecycle of the application, from developing and testing to deploying. In this way, these engineers cultivate a variety of skills that is not restricted to a certain function. There might be tight integration between security teams, operations and development all through the application lifecycle.

Role of a DevOps Engineer

Currently, the DevOps engineer role differs from one company to another. Smaller companies may search for engineers with broader responsibilities and skillsets. For instance, the job description possibly will call for product implementation together with software development. Other smaller companies that have many developers but a smaller number of people that can understand the technical infrastructure, will possibly search for applicants with advanced experience in system administration. Larger companies may search for a DevOps engineer for a certain phase of the DevOps lifecycle, that will operate a specific automation tool. Other larger or possibly older companies with a strong system administration foundation will presumably search for applicant that has extensive experience in operations and software development.

The rudimentary and standard duties of a DevOps engineer are:

- Collaborates with system administrators, operation managers and developers; implement processes they are in charge of, and take part in building IT infrastructure. All steps starting from practical analysis to application deployment and monitoring is taken care of, with the objective to augment general system scalability and reliability. Accomplishing this via consistent and periodic interaction and communication with the teams involved when troubleshooting software and applications; they similarly monitor performance and cost-effectiveness requirement.
- Responsible for IT infrastructure administration and upkeep, which encompasses governance over cloud data storage, remote and virtual resources, storages, network, software

and hardware. Makes sure of conformity to principles by monitoring the company's online websites and software. The DevOps engineer also standardizes processes and tools in the team and induces their synchronized evolution and enhancement. In addition, they keenly improve and build platform services, applications and website software; as well as manage and host databases. They monitor and check alerts on a regular basis, examine and identify root causes; install preemptive processes to prevent problems from reoccurring, as well as thorough responsibility and ownership of the company's web service performance; certifies application deployment in scalable architecture while conducting capacity planning.

- Develops and designs the company's infrastructure and its architecture. The DevOps engineer enables automated risk-management strategies by creating, testing and deploying those strategies; they maintain company's deployment and configuration tools such as *Terraform* and *Puppet.*

- Helps in advancement of knowledge distribution and entire DevOps culture all through the department; stays up-to-date on industry best practices and trends whilst identifying prospects for design development, automation and other options in an understandable manner to increase operational efficiency.

- Writes documentation and specifications for server-side components.

- Handles script writing for continuous integration and continuous deployment.

Essential Skills for a DevOps Engineer

In most organizations, the following paragraphs highlights the skills required of a DevOps engineer.

- **Education**

  A degree in Information Science, Computer Science, Engineering and other related fields are appropriate credentials for this role. Experience matching with the fields previously stated are also considered. This encompasses experience as a system administrator, developer or any other member of a DevOps-focused team.

- **Automation tool experience**

  Automation tools such as *Docker, Nagios, Jenkins, GitHub, Fabric,*

Ansible, Puppet, Chef, and so on, all play a key part when it has to do with automation. Knowledge of these tools is highly desirable by IT companies. Handling automation is one of the aspects that differentiates a DevOps engineer from a Linux engineer. DevOps engineers must be up-to-date on the latest tools that can help to improve efficiency.

- **Technical skills**

  A DevOps engineer needs to have programming experience to incorporate coding and scripting, in addition to the knowledge of off-the-shelf tools. Coding skills may encompass Ruby, PHP, Python, C++, C#, java etc., while scripting skills generally involve the knowledge of PowerShell or bash scripts. A DevOps engineer position in most companies entails experience with cloud coding languages, automation and integration technology. Database administrators, IT project managers or systems managers, to mention a few potential career paths, can acquire this experience. Because DevOps engineers focus on writing code to alter current cloud platforms instead of creating new ones, companies that practice DevOps deploy code with more precision and more often than their competitors. In other words, a potential DevOps engineer should have extensive knowledge of technology utilized by DevOps engineers as well as experience in various open source technologies. These include

- o Source control (for example *VSTS, Bitbucket, Git* etc.)
- o Orchestration (for example *Swarm, Mesos, Kubernetes* etc.)

- Open source OS
- Infrastructure automation (for example *Ansible, Chef, Puppet*)
- Deployment orchestration and automation (for example *Octopus Deploy, VSTS, Jenkins*)
- Continuous integration (for example *VSTS, Bamboo, Jenkins*)
- Container concepts (for example *Docker, LXD*)
- Cloud technology (for example *OpenStack, Google Cloud Platform, Azure, AWS*)
- Agile project management.

On a normal workday, DevOps engineers explores different components of the cloud environment and create code to scale those components and meet immediate business requirements. Some of these actions involves adding full objects that act like containers, inserting or modifying workflow processes, creating permissions or inserting users to a cloud setup. Their attention should be on support, optimization, documentation and configuration of infrastructure modules. This would entail the capability to create small code snippets or rapid-fire coding in multiple languages. Signifying that DevOps engineers must be experienced with testing in a virtual environment. The skill to organizing insertions and integrations across various systems is what differentiates the DevOps engineer from a Cloud Database Manager.

The capability to create secure code is a huge asset in DevOps. DevOps engineers are responsible for aiding the users of the systems they create, and the initial line of defense is to guard the cloud against viruses and hackers. They ensure this by creating secure software from the beginning. The DevOps engineer, with collaboration between them to improve a company's infrastructure security procedures, might supervise the DevSecOps team. The DevSecOps team is formed on the basis that all practices in a company requires security measures. The team participates in continuous testing and monitoring across the platforms, searches for vulnerabilities, and promotes comprehension of business practices.

- **Knowledge of database systems**
  A DevOps engineer handles data processing at the deployment phase, necessitating experience with either NoSQL or SQL database models.
- **Communication and interpersonal skills**

Even though a DevOps engineer should be skilled in technical aspects, they should also have excellent communication skills. They must make sure that the team operates successfully, gets and provides feedback to maintain continuous delivery. The result – a product – relies on their capability to communicate with team members. Although the exigencies of a DevOps engineer may sometimes need her or him to work alone, they must be strong collaborators. This is because this role needs them to expand on the efforts of other team members to assign tenants, develop workflow processes, scale cloud programs and more. It is common for a DevOps engineer to be asked to guide architecture teams and software developers inside a company, to impart to them on the ways to create scalable software. In addition, they work with security and IT teams to make certain of quality releases. There are some DevOps teams that involve DevSecOps, wherein proactive security measures are applied to DevOps principles. The DevOps engineer is an essential part of the team since they work with in-house clients. This comprises of project managers, application and software developers, QC personnel and project stakeholders mostly from inside the same company. Although it is rare for them to work with outside users or clients, they maintain a "client first" mindset to meet the requirements of internal clients. Interpersonal skills are essential to the entire success of a DevOps engineer, since achieving common ground amongst teams is not usually a simple task. Rather, it needs persistent communication. DevOps engineers should be confident communicating easily and clearly to pass their message fully.

Chapter 3

DevOps and Security: Mitigating Threats

Before the introduction of DevOps, companies carried out their application's security checks during the last phases of the software development lifecycle. This was due to the focus mostly centered on application development. When engineers finally execute security checks, the software would have been near to completion. Noticing security issues at such a long-overdue phase meant tons of code rework, which is a time-consuming and laborious task. Predictably, patching became the favored solution.

IT infrastructure has experienced enormous deviations in recent years. The move to cloud computing, shared resources and dynamic provisioning have driven advantages surrounding cost, agility and IT speed, thus assisting in enhancing software development. The capacity for deploying software in the cloud has improved both speed and scale, the shift to DevOps processes and agile practices made "big bang" software deployment an action of the past. Specifically, DevOps – the principle of combining IT operations and development as one team – has aided with a lot, from increased component releases to better application stability. However, numerous compliance monitoring and security tools have not kept pace with these deviations, as they were not created to assess code at the rate DevOps needs. This has confirmed the interpretation that security is the largest obstacle to quick software development, and more largely IT innovation. Hackers are always searching for best techniques to set up malware and other attacks. An example here would be a successful malware insertion to an application during the build process, that went undetected before been sent to customers. This would lead to lots of damage for both the customers and the company involved. Executing DevSecOps has an undeviating positive effect, since it assists to manage possibly devastating issues.

Chapter 4

DevSecOps

DevSecOps is a method of undertaking IT security on the principle that all persons involved in the software development lifecycle is accountable for security, hence integrating security functions to development and operations. DevSecOps is a crucial and expected response to the issues brought about by legacy security systems on the contemporary continuous delivery pipeline. The aim is to connect the outdated gaps between security and IT while making sure of quick and secure code delivery. Thinking in silos is superseded by shared accountability of security tasks and increased communication all through the stages of the delivery process. In DevSecOps, secure code and rate of delivery are integrated into one restructured process. Aligning with agile lean approach, security testing is done iteratively without slowing down the delivery cycles. Serious security problems are handled proactively.

Benefits of Implementing DevSecOps

Security procedures that are a part of the development process permits security and DevOps professionals as a team to cultivate the strengths of agile methodologies without hindering the objective of developing secure code. The safety measures intrinsic in DevSecOps has many benefits. These are:

- Enhanced Return on Investment (ROI) in current security systems and better operational proficiencies through security and other parts of IT.
- Capability to utilize cloud services comprehensively. For instance, companies operating resources in the Amazon Web Services (AWS) cloud

obtain growth in detective and preventive security mechanisms inside the continuous deployment and integration system of AWS. While even more companies depend on cloud technologies to maintain processes, autonomous security efforts remain critical to avoid expensive downtimes.

- Early discovery of weaknesses in code.
- More chances for quality assurance testing and automated builds.
- Improved communication and collaboration among teams.
- Quick response to requirements and changes.
- Better agility and speed for security teams.

Important DevSecOps Keynotes

Not all DevSecOps process are the same. DevSecOps is a journey the company is undertaking. During this journey, there is a realization that various teams are at varying stages down the path. The keynotes below are guideposts that a company can utilize to aid in decision making during the journey.

- **Continuous security**

    Like continuous deployment and continuous integration, continuous security involves the tackling of security testing and issues in the Continuous Delivery pipeline. The best practices for continuous security are:

    o Precise record of every software version and package information recorded through infrastructure as code. Carry out automated searches to find out if any of the packages contain recognized CVEs linked in it, and then plan corrective actions.

o The integration of security tools into the CI/CD pipeline.

o Automated security processes in order not to obstruct DevOps agility.

o Measurements from production security technologies like Runtime Application Self-Protection (RASP) and Web Application Firewall (WAF) sent back to developers to enact application updates.

o Regular or periodic planned external penetration tests for carrying out deep-dive analysis.

o Source code for important trademarks on test or build systems retrieved only by authorized users. Test and build scripts should not include credentials to any machine that has trade secrets.

o Embrace well-established infrastructure approaches to confirm that production systems are in place.

- **Visibility of security**
In most companies, security tasks are untracked, unknown and hidden. Ultimately, the significance of security is sometimes not simple to comprehend. DevSecOps allow for measuring, tasking and tracking of small security tasks, just as some other forms of work.

- **Empowering engineering teams**
There is empowerment of operations and development as they deploy secure

software into production themselves. Security professionals offer support as toolsmiths or coaches but are not chiefly accountable for security. Make certain that processes and tools are created for operations and developers, not security professionals.

- **Security as Code**

  Security tasks, especially testing, are converted from a labor-intensive procedure for security professionals into configurations, test cases and tools that can be tested uninterruptedly all through the software lifecycle. Security as Code involves developing security into DevOps practices and tools, making it a vital piece of the workflows and tool chains. This is done by surveying how modifications to infrastructure and code are made and discovering areas to insert security gates, tests and checks without causing needless delays or costs.

- **Prevent and protect**
  The perfect code might never be created, nor will all attackers be stopped or detected. However, the top security tactics include a balance of runtime protection in the course of operations (SecOps) and secure coding in the course of development (DevSec).

- **Shift Left**
  This denotes that security tasks start sooner, in the course of development, and continue for the duration of the software development lifecycle, with continual feedback at all phases from development to production. This concept does not indicate that security is finished in the course of development.

The objective of shifting left is to minimize the length of time needed to test, increase quality, and diminish the risk of security challenges after the cycle concludes, when it is very time-consuming and expensive to resolve issues. Previously, development teams have been slightly hesitant to shift left due to the worry that working with security staffs too soon in the process would lead to complications and delays. Nevertheless, the world of DevOps has improved intensely in the last decade, and shifting left is quickly turning into a best practice in the domain of security and DevOps.

Getting Started with DevSecOps

A company's technical and cultural transfer to DevSecOps process would help deal with security risks more successfully immediately. It is necessary to regard security professionals as beneficial assets that aid in minimizing downtimes instead of been viewed as a limitation to agility. For instance, quick discovery of a badly developed software that is not capable of scaling in the cloud saves computing costs, resources and time. Scalability in the cloud involves inserting security standards on a greater scale. Administration of system builds and continuous threat modeling, is required while technology-driven companies progress at a quick rate.

There is preparation needed before updating the pipelines. To begin, there is need for complete understanding of what potentially makes the company's applications vulnerable. A general technique is threat modelling to aid in defining attack vectors, vulnerabilities and possible threats. The length of time taken here will help determine the security checks the company will carry out as part of the process. Secure coding procedures is another important factor. This includes identifying the tools used to support the process and the notifications policy for when there is a deviation, peer review strategies by the development team to sustain the process, suitable coding standards, and attack simulation to direct on the applications (based on threat model). Below are different forms of security initiatives in Continuous Delivery phases.

- **Commit**

  This phase involves the development actions performed before code is checked in to the repository, and is handled by the developer. Main actions for the developer include:

  - Peer-review by having other developers check the code for

mistakes and to know if it followed approved secure coding principles.

o Static Code Analysis implemented by the developer inside the available development environment. With this, there is early detection of security problems and bugs before codes are committed, hence, producing the fastest feedback.

o Evaluate and modify the threat model. Perform checks to see if the new changes require extra security checks or increase the application's area of attack or possible abuse cases.

- **Build**

This phase can be regarded as the automated form of the Continuous

Integration phase. Rapid analysis is capitalized on to identify issues overlooked by the developer and give quick feedback. These actions include:

- o Unit checks in addition to the already existing functional unit checks, to assist vulnerability checks and the availability of appropriate countermeasures in the code.

- o Progressive Source Code Analysis of the new changes with notifications triggered for high-risk changes. Aside from notifications, this offers reporting in order to analyze the entire health of the present source branch.

- o Clean builds with no warnings or failures. Existing warnings in builds need to be reviewed and resolved or acknowledged and blocked on a case-by-case condition.

- o Code coverage review, unit tests might not cover the entirety of the code base, so monitoring is necessary to make sure it is very close.

- **Test**

  This phase is sometimes referred to as integration testing where the software is deployed to a clean test environment utilizing similar deployment automation like that of production. Preferably, majority of the integration and functional testing for the software takes place in this phase with automated test scripts. These actions include:

  - o Certain integration and functional security testing will validate

certain abuse cases as outlined by
the threat model.

o Focused dynamic scanning that
examines the weakest areas of the
software with largest risk, based
on the threat model.

o Security smoke tests to unmask
issues found in deployment and
configuration.

o Automated security attacks using
existing tools to exercise general
types of attack against several
forms of services and applications.

o Use manual pen testing, fuzz
testing or deep static analysis
infrequently or as needed.

- **Deploy**
In this phase, the secured application is
set up. The activities to carry out here
include:

- o Validating runtime asserts through stochastic automated unit tests.
- o Performing an additional security smoke test to unmask issues found in deployment and configuration.
- o Feedback/monitoring of the application and environment. Make certain logging is established and functional.
- o Postmortems of the entire cycle to find out if anything went wrong, if any security issues were identified and resolved, and how to make improvements.

Developing a DevSecOps pipeline

This pipeline encompasses the group of processes and tools that continually execute security activities as code is developed, incorporated, tested, deployed and in use. Even though there is mainly a single delivery pipeline, integrating a security viewpoint of the pipeline will aid in comprehending the security cost flow, illuminating gridlocks and stimulating confidence in the outcome. The pipeline covers the entire lifecycle, managing both the attacks in operations and the weaknesses in development. The objective of integrating security to the pipeline is to offer susceptibility details to the development team immediately, via the tools currently in use. As the process progresses to operations, the aim is to show visibility of the attacker, attempted attack vectors, targeted systems, and success or failure of preventive measures.

The foremost sequence in the DevSecOps pipeline consist of integrations with operations and development tools, an analytics core, and security tools. The measurements from these tools supplies into an analytics system for alerts, reviews and chronological tracking. Some of these events are:

- Software architecture specifics.
- Attacks on general code weaknesses.
- Recognized exposures in frameworks and libraries.
- General code vulnerabilities.
- Application record of all frameworks and libraries.
- Attacks on frameworks and libraries.

Executing an alert infrastructure motivates downstream security participants (executives, audit, operations, testers, developers etc.) to perform jointly with upstream support (such as security testers) to make certain that task is augmented for them. The DevSecOps pipeline should have extremely close feedback loops, like in a matter of seconds. The quicker the feedback gets to those that require it, the more profitable and secure the DevSecOps pipeline will be. At the beginning, the DevSecOps pipeline will simply confirm little aspects of the application. However, as time goes on, and problems are fixed there is a gradual increase in automation of security defenses and strategies. In the long term, the objective is to move from labor-intensive security testing to a completely automated pipeline proficient in deploying safe code into production.

Customarily, DevSecOps prefers the utilization of alerts to PDF reports. Nevertheless, PDF reports may be produced for a few occasions like compliance. Alerts inform teams that requires security event notification straightaway via the existing tools, as a regular routine. Different analytics system may be needed for threat and vulnerabilities event, grouped as:

- **Alerts**

The objective is to send information about attacks, probes, fixes, misconfigurations, general code weaknesses, and new CVEs to the team that requires them via existing tools. This involves integrations and plugins for tools like *Pivotal, Azure, AWS, IntelliJ, Eclipse, Splunk, Maven, Gradle, VictorOps, PagerDuty, ArcSight, Jenkins, GitHub, JIRA, Kubernete*s and *Docker.*

- **Sensors**

  Attack detection and security testing can be categorized as sensors, used for monitoring software development systems and organizations. The best sensors offer quick response, very high accuracy, and operates constantly. Sensors can be custom rules; fixed rules in protection or analysis technology, custom built test cases, and so on.

- **Security Analytics**

  Every measurement detail received from sensors on attacks, vulnerabilities, libraries, inventory etc., should be saved, calculated and monitored long term. A tool created to reinforce a DevSecOps pipeline is preferable; other options could be a custom database or a spreadsheet. The model analytics repository offers amazing reporting, supervises alert rules, and monitors problems (both attacks and vulnerabilities) long term.

DevSecOps Best Practices

DevSecOps effects a truly agile perspective to security, disintegrating huge security activities into incremental enhancements that are handled as usual development activities. These few sets of tasks involve continuous integration, to facilitate security builds in the long term rather than continually starting all over. After ascertaining the subsequent security issue, a standard engineering procedure can work on the enhancement. The continuous pressure between building defenses and endeavoring to disintegrate them truly makes companies more secure. The quicker the DevSecOps cycle is repeated, the quicker security is improved. After some time, there will be a totally developed security system that will deliver assurance within and outside the company. Below are some best practices that will aid in the smooth running of a DevSecOps process:

- **Find the most serious security issue**
  When making the decision on the next task, the team examines every possible security task existing and makes it evident. The team might resolve

vulnerabilities/defects, create an architectural enhancement, reduce some technical debt, insert additional features or work on refining the team's practices or tools used for productivity, security or quality improvement. It is necessary for the team to utilize their developed security architecture and threat model to make a knowledgeable decision regarding the next serious security issues. They should examine the business cost for some specific threats and the business cost for executing preemptive measures for those threats. Data from external and internal sources should be used to fathom next steps for efficiently minimizing risk.

If there is no security architecture or a threat model, then the company must begin with evaluating risks across the whole application stack (network, container and cloud, libraries and framework, and applications and APIs) plus creating a system architecture diagram.

- **Execute a defense plan**

  The team needs to erect a defense strategy after making the decision on the security issue to handle. A defense strategy is more than one security product or mechanism; it can incorporate procedural controls, background checks, training, supporting procedures, secure coding implementations, technical security systems and so on. The defense strategy for a single issue can include more than one crucial defense and a group of secondary defenses. DevSecOps allows for continuous reprioritizing of the existing defenses and threat. The capability for fast responses is essential for a world of ever-changing threats. The task of truly executing the defense approach does not have to be unique and conveyed as configuration or code in source control. Regulating security in this manner increases the possibility of testing and redeployment whenever, making certain that defenses are adequately configured, operating as it should, and defenses established.

The team should record every defense approach for operation in a JIRA ticket that envelopes every security development in progress. This would include:

o   Security testing strategies.

o   Functioning procedures on use of the defenses, operation and configuration. This should apply to operations team members, end users, and developers.

- o Defense scenario on the workings of the defense strategy. It should visibly show the way the threat is resolved and the reason for the effectiveness of the defense.
- o Issue description.

- **Automate security testing**

  DevSecOps makes sure of adequately operated, configured, and implemented defense strategies. Security testing is the method to confirm that existing security approach equal envisioned defenses. In DevSecOps, there is effort on automating those tests through Security as Code, in order to execute them frequently without human interaction (especially security professionals) in the critical route. There are many tools for automating security verification of a system. Below are aspects to consider when deciding on the tools to acquire or use:

- o Tools utilized for security testing differs a lot in their capability to examine actual applications for a wide range of problems. Trying out the tool is the only method to check the productiveness of that tool on the company's APIs and applications. Set up the environment in such a way that it detects only actual vulnerabilities without flagging false alarms.

- o Focus on the whole process to find out if the tool needs human interaction to operate or configure, and if it needs a professional to deduce and classify the outcome. The goal here is to eradicate human participation in the critical route, in order to deliver code to production with assurance and speed.

- o The adoption of any tool comprises of complete batch of integrations, extra process phases, and a team to deduce, operate and configure. Select strong platforms that enables handling of various forms of security issues utilizing an integrated architecture.

- **Identify attacks and prevent exploits**

  Companies that adopt DevSecOps assume a well-adjusted technique that centers on reducing weaknesses in the course of development; and on discovering and thwarting weaknesses from exploitation in production. Even though these events have conventionally been separated, DevOps has combined them as DevSecOps projects maintain the entire application lifecycle. The categories for the tools aimed at identifying attacks and thwarting exploits are:

- o Security Information and Event Management (SIEM) tools offers insight to real-time review of security notifications produced by network hardware and applications, and are essential to managing attacks in DevSecOps. Examples include *ArcSight* and *Splunk*.
- o Intrusion Detection and Prevention systems offers various host, container and network level defenses against attack. The company's standard technology stack should regulate and install the tools selected. Examples include *Kismet* and *Snort*.

o Web Application Firewall have some known challenges like spotty defense and difficult configuration. However, companies can still use it as a structure for virtual patches or for basic defense in a DevSecOps project. Examples include *Imperva* and *ModSecurity*.

o Runtime Application Self-Protection utilizes software components to add exploit prevention and attack detection directly to software irrespective of deployment method or location. Projects in DevSecOps utilize RASP to achieve targeted attack blocking and the adaptability of simple deployments in container or cloud environments. Examples include *Prevoty* and *Immunio*.

- **Verify code dependencies**

  There is an increase in software created externally, open source or off-the-shelf. Hence, companies should inspect these features the same way as the internal code inspection. This is specifically important as numerous software regarded as internal are comprised of third-party assets and libraries. Moreover, many external applications do not meet IT security criterions, signifying that they may contain vulnerabilities and easily exploited.

- **Create metrics**

  A company can monitor its risk or threat management through a well-established method of measurement. It discloses if the company is discovering fewer defects in the long term and if it is taking less or more time to discover these defects. In order to have a complete picture of its application security, a company should frequently verify its asset coverage and other performance standards like vulnerability acceptance and the ratio of surface area coverage by manual versus automated testing. Significant enhancement is questionable without accurately evaluating the current situation.

- **Educate employees on secure coding**

Chapter 5

Conclusion

DevOps evolved from agile methodology. It is a combination of developers and operators. It is more than that though since the objective of DevOps is to create a culture of open communication and collaboration, to enhance deployment rate, realize quicker time-to-market, reduce the frequency of failure of new releases, reduce lead-time between resolutions, and enhance average time-to-delivery. The lifecycle of DevOps includes continuous development, continuous testing, continuous integration, continuous delivery, continuous deployment, and continuous monitoring. DevOps offers many benefits to the business including an improved internal culture as well as quality and speed. There are several factors to put into consideration when getting ready to implement DevOps; these are visualization, automation, determining expected outcome, and formal processes. For best practices, the company should explore various deployment strategies to find out the one they find comfortable. In addition, breaking down silos, automation and proficient tool selection are other best practices. Transitioning from a software developer or a system administrator to a DevOps engineer requires knowledge of the role a DevOps engineer assumes, and the skills expected.

DevSecOps involves injecting security right from the very start of the DevOps process (development) to the deployment and monitoring phases. It offers so many benefits like early discovery of weaknesses in code, more chances for quality assurance testing and automated builds, improved communication and collaboration among teams, quick response to requirements and changes, and better agility and speed for security teams. Getting started with DevSecOps involves applying security to the various forms of continuous delivery. Developing a DevSecOps pipeline encompasses setting up different monitoring systems grouped as security analytics, sensors, and alerts. DevSecOps best practices involves discovering threats, educating employees on secure coding, creating metrics, verifying code dependencies, identifying attacks and thwart exploits, automating security testing, and executing a defense plan.

Finito di scrivere nel mese di gennaio 2015
Stampato e venduto da **amazon**

www.ingramcontent.com/pod-product-compliance
Lightning Source LLC
LaVergne TN
LVHW042351060326
832902LV00006B/537